BEST. WIFE. EVER.

FOR: ______________________

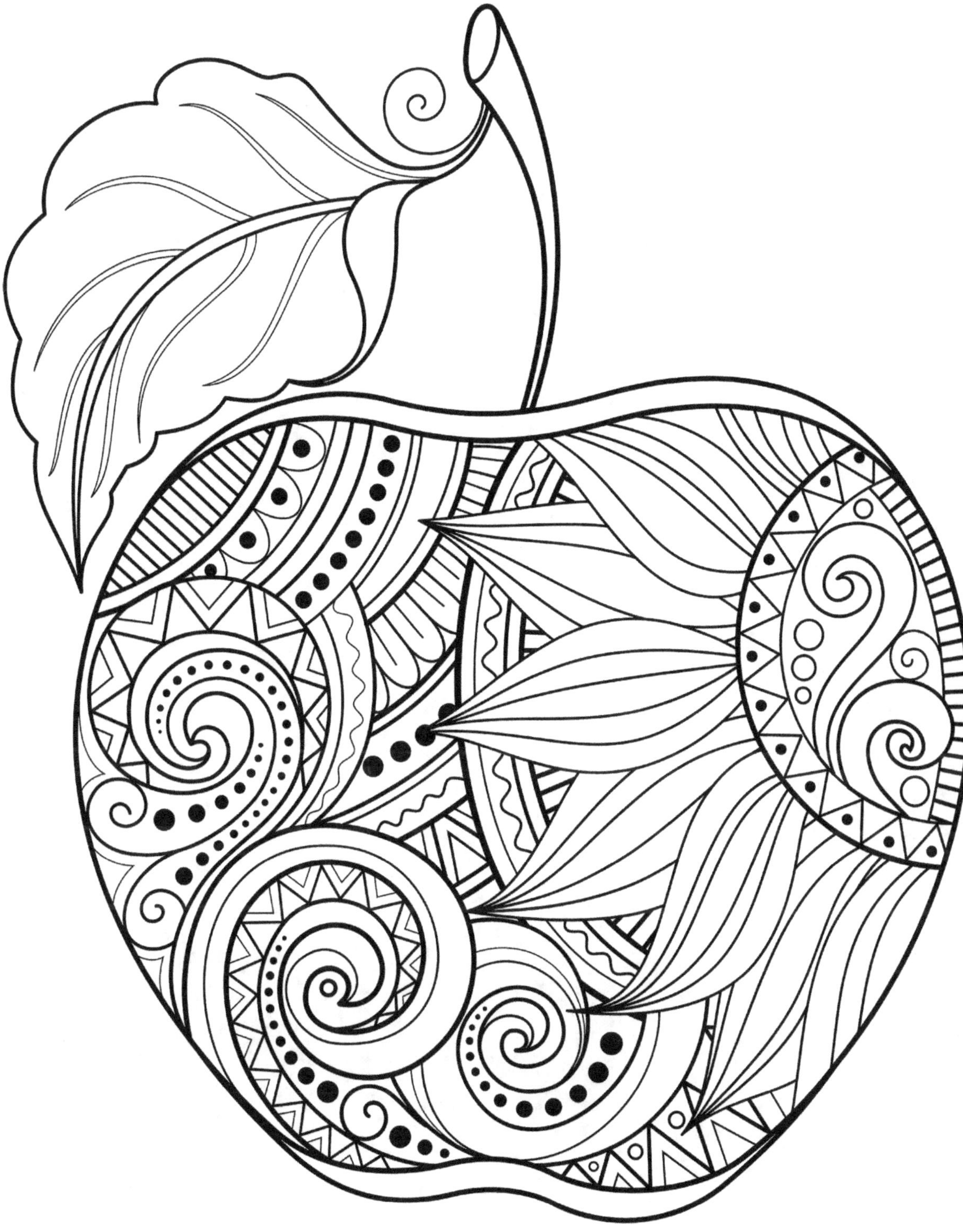

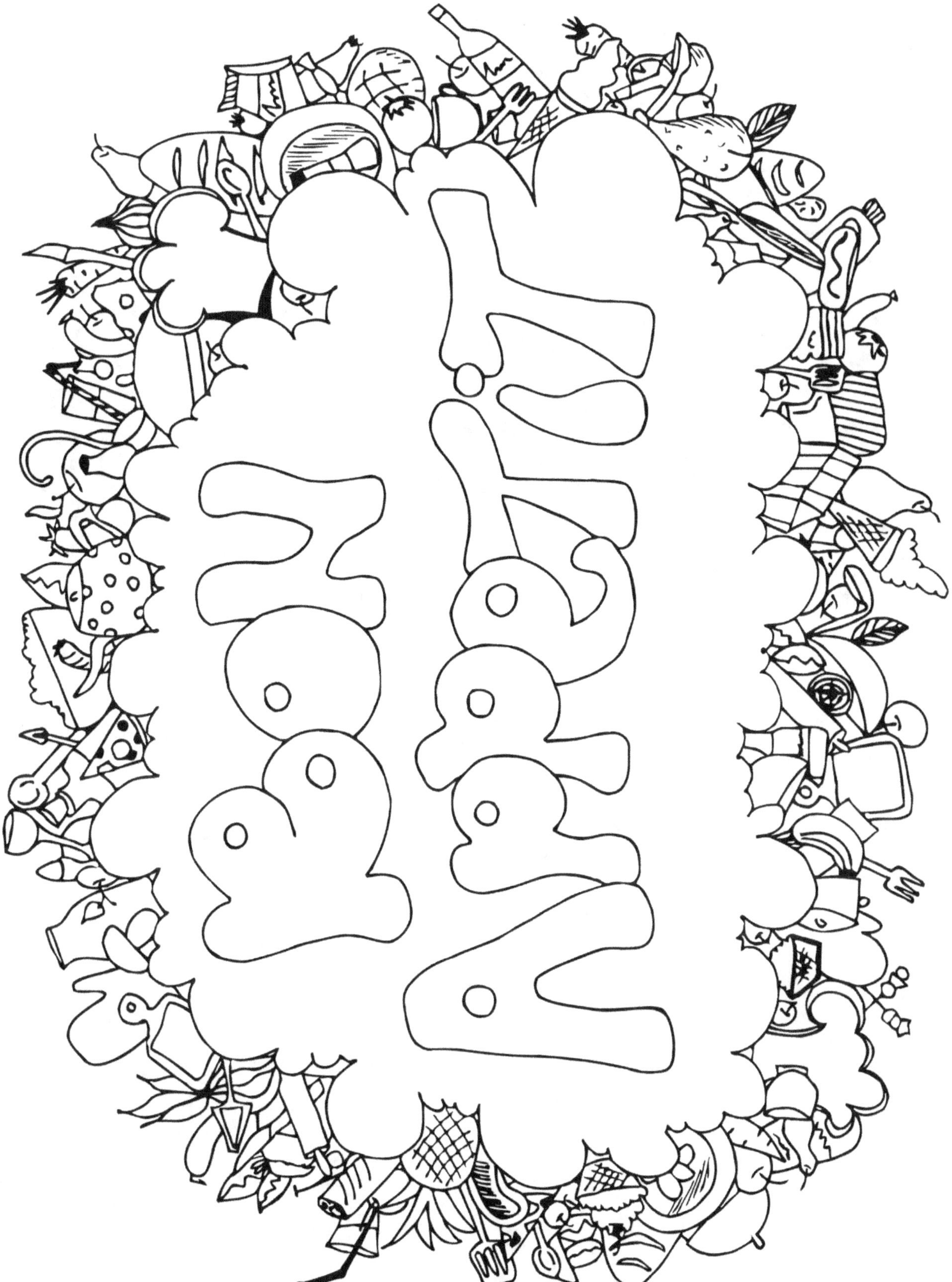
BON
APPETIT

TEA

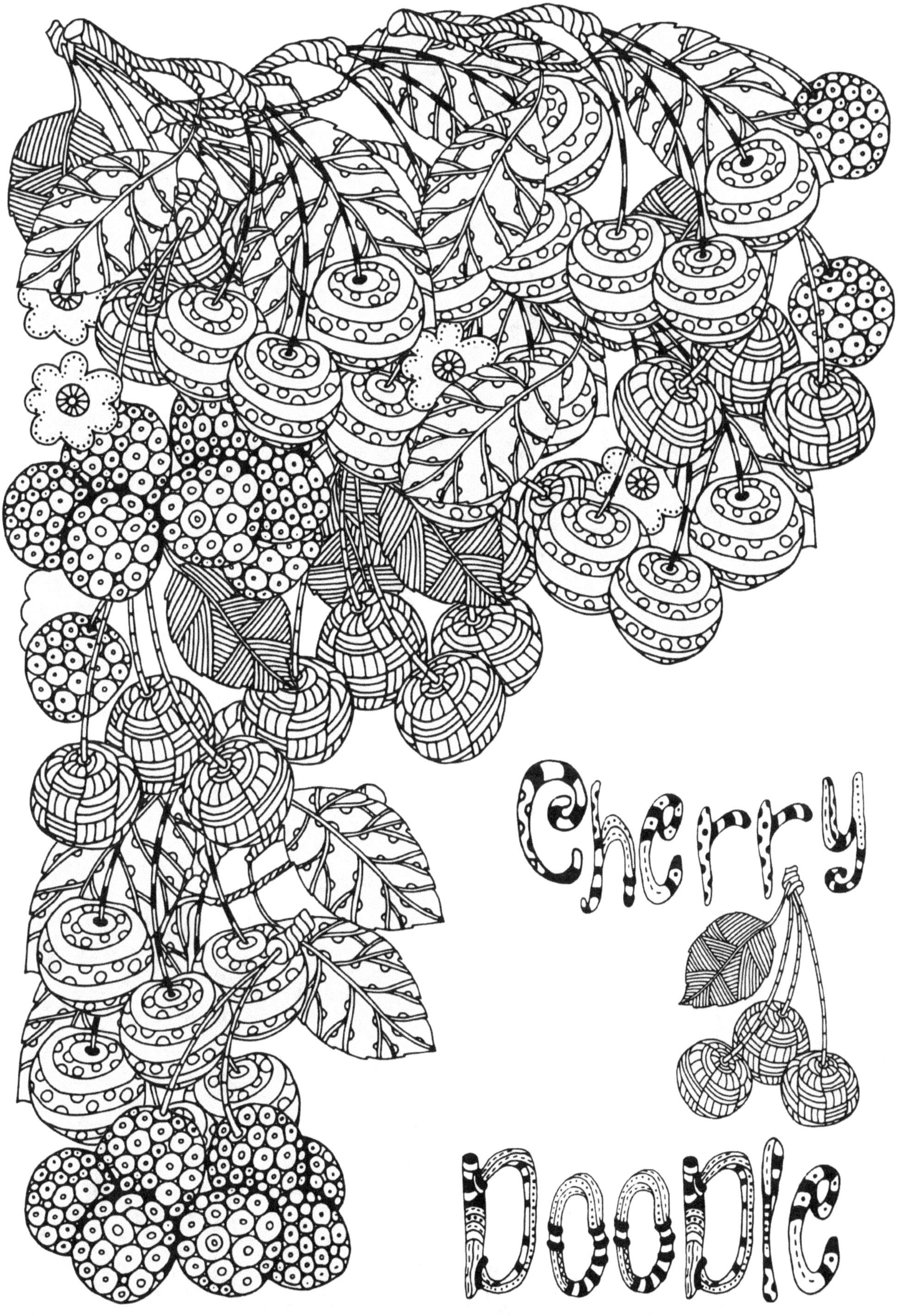

Cherry
Doodle

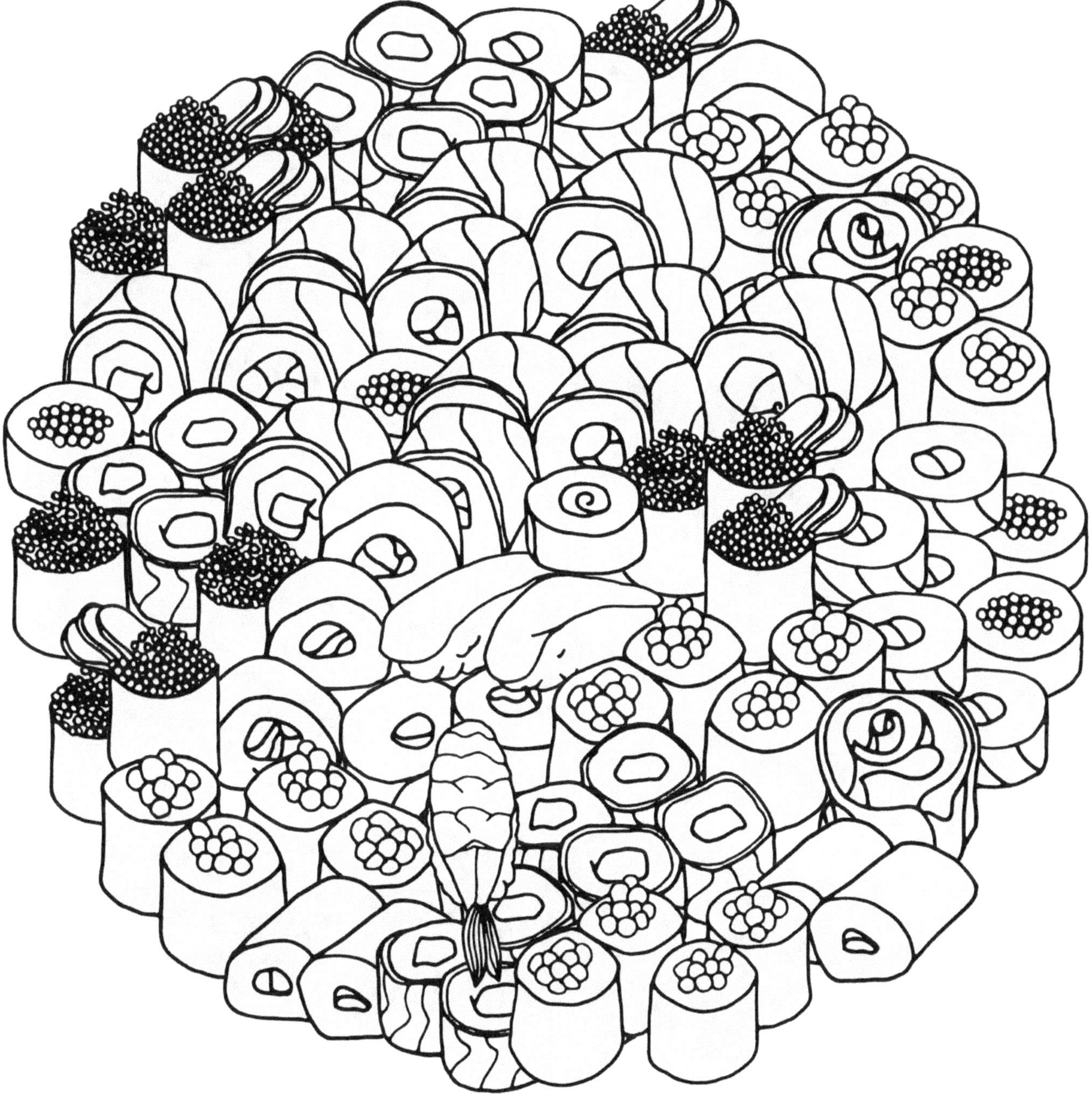

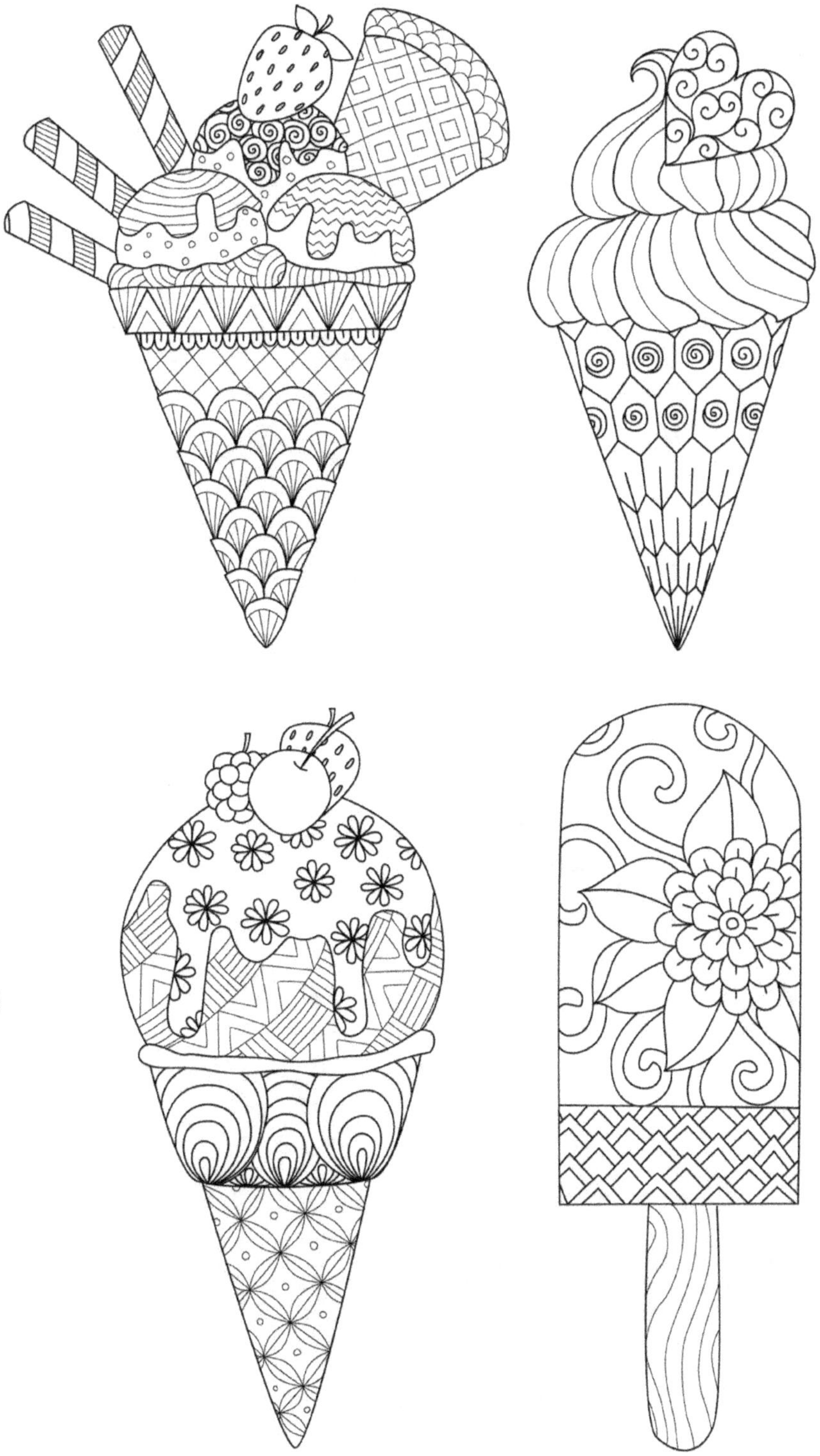

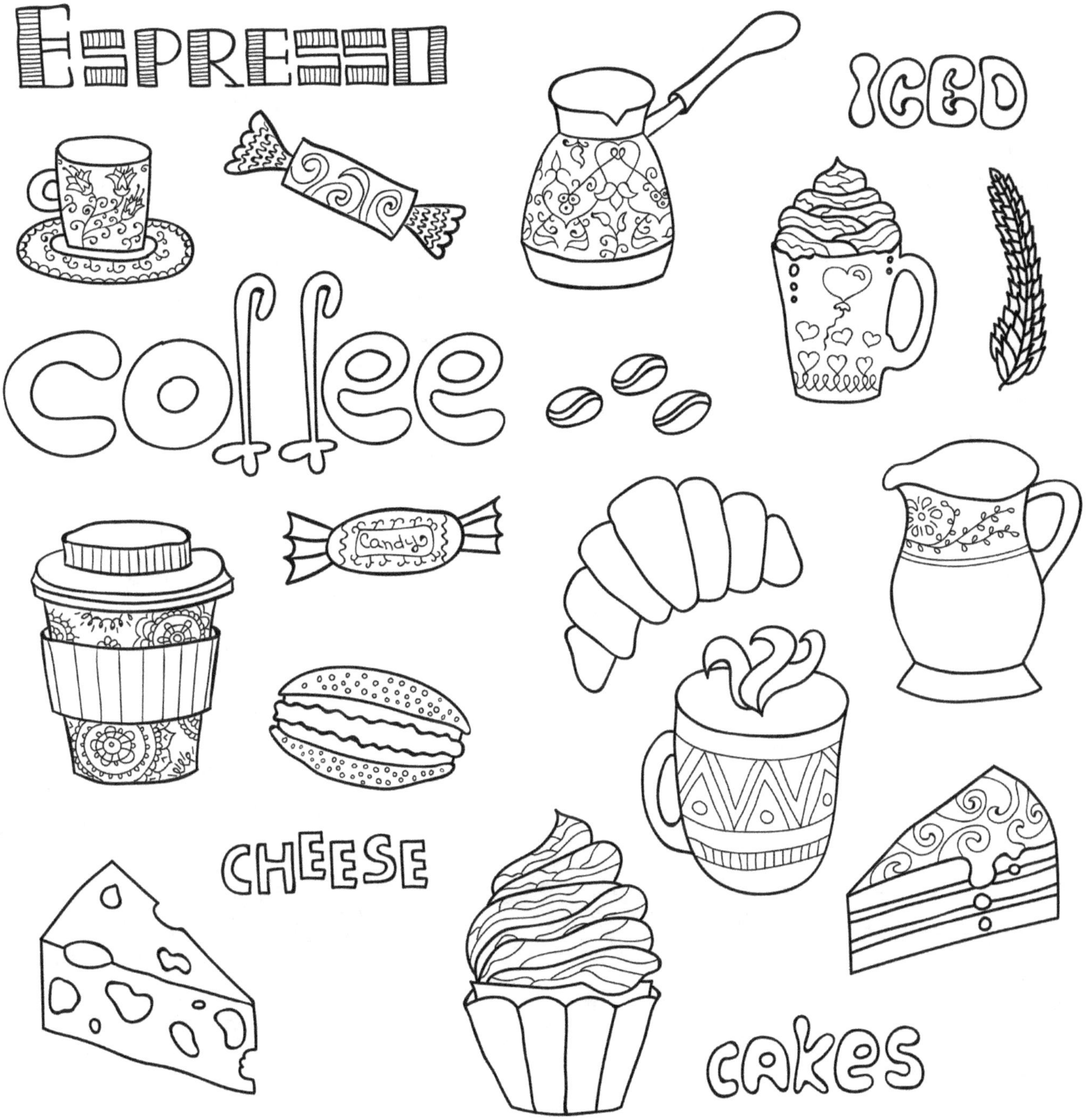
Espresso
ICED
coffee
Candy
CHEESE
cakes

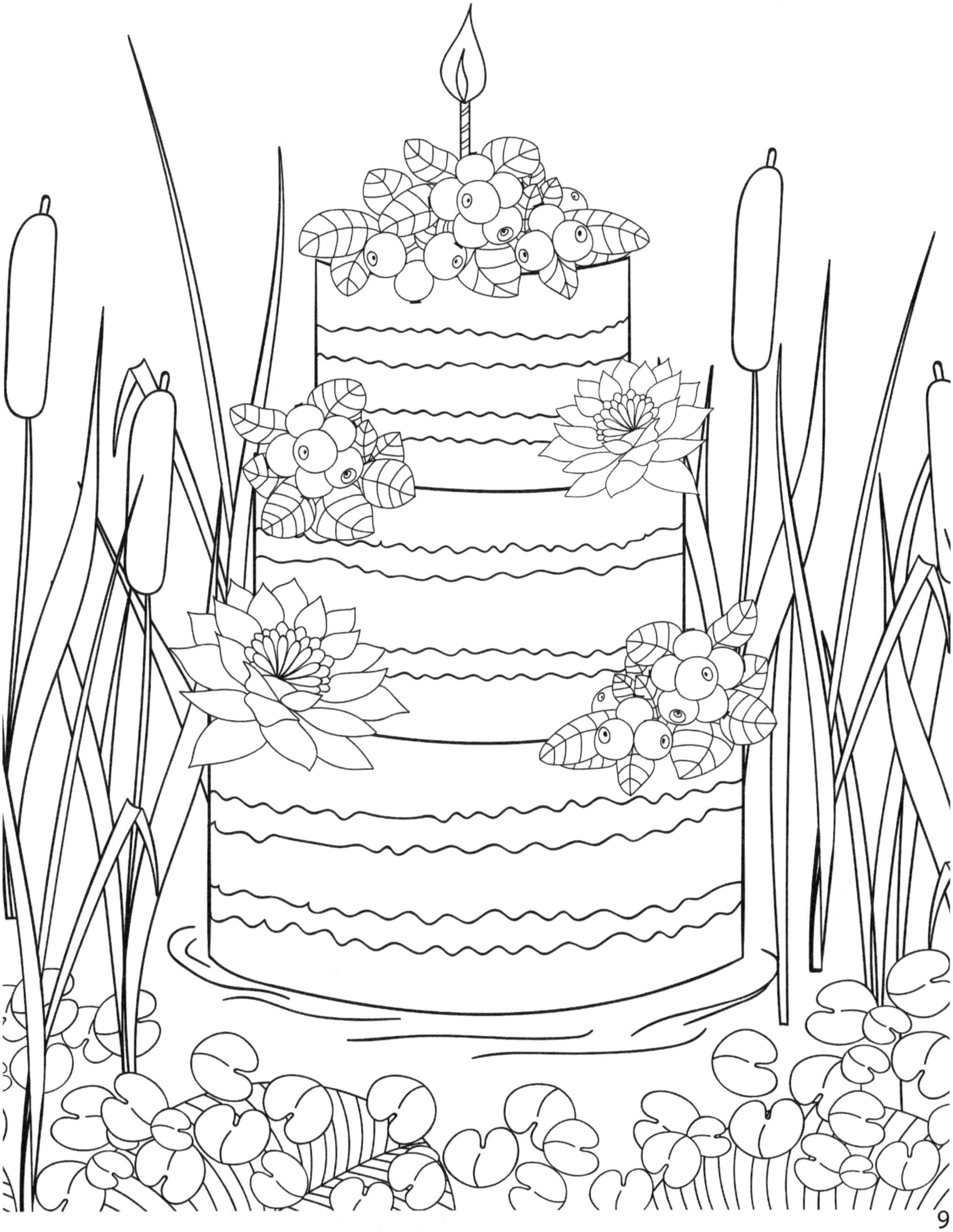

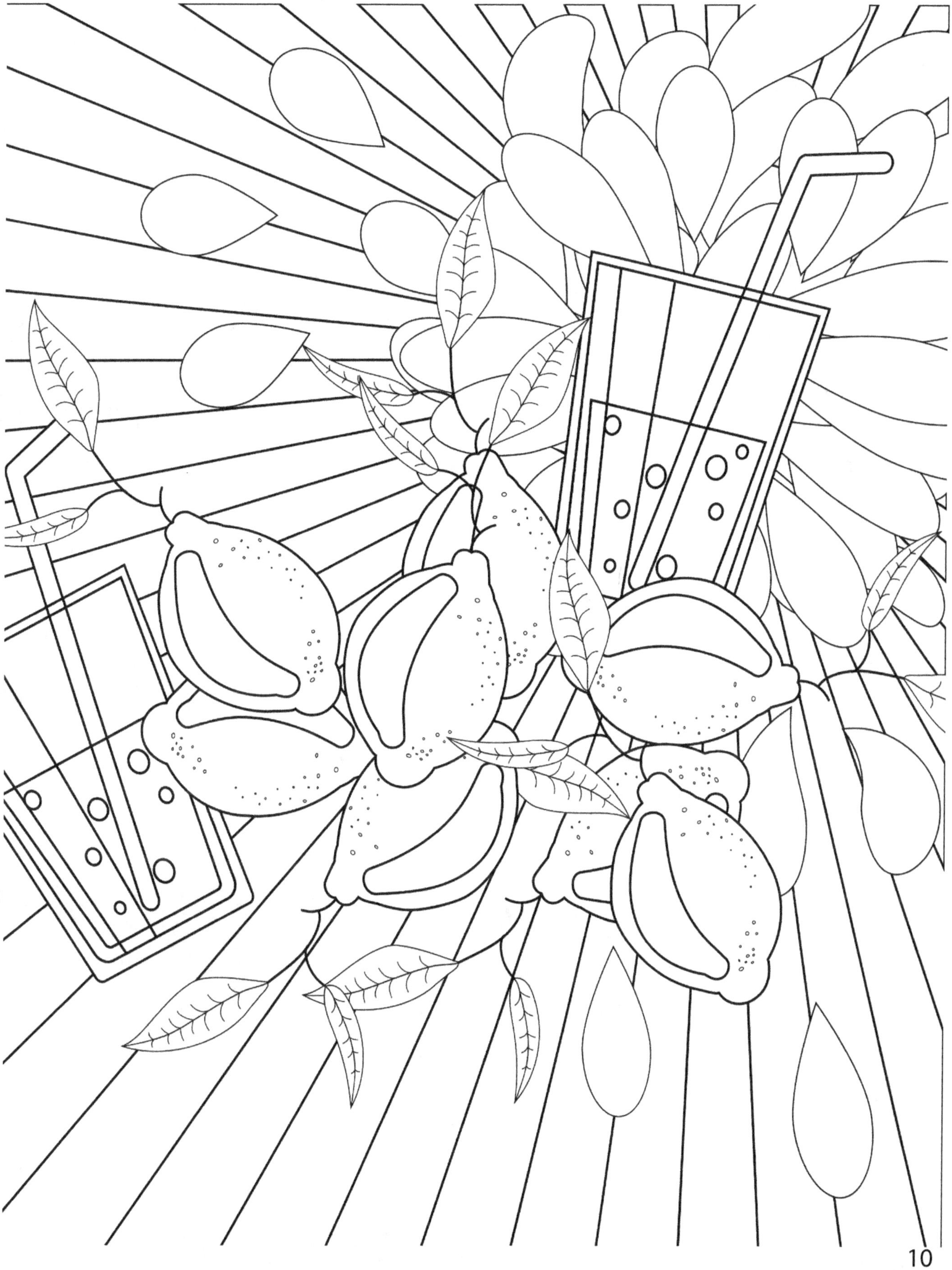

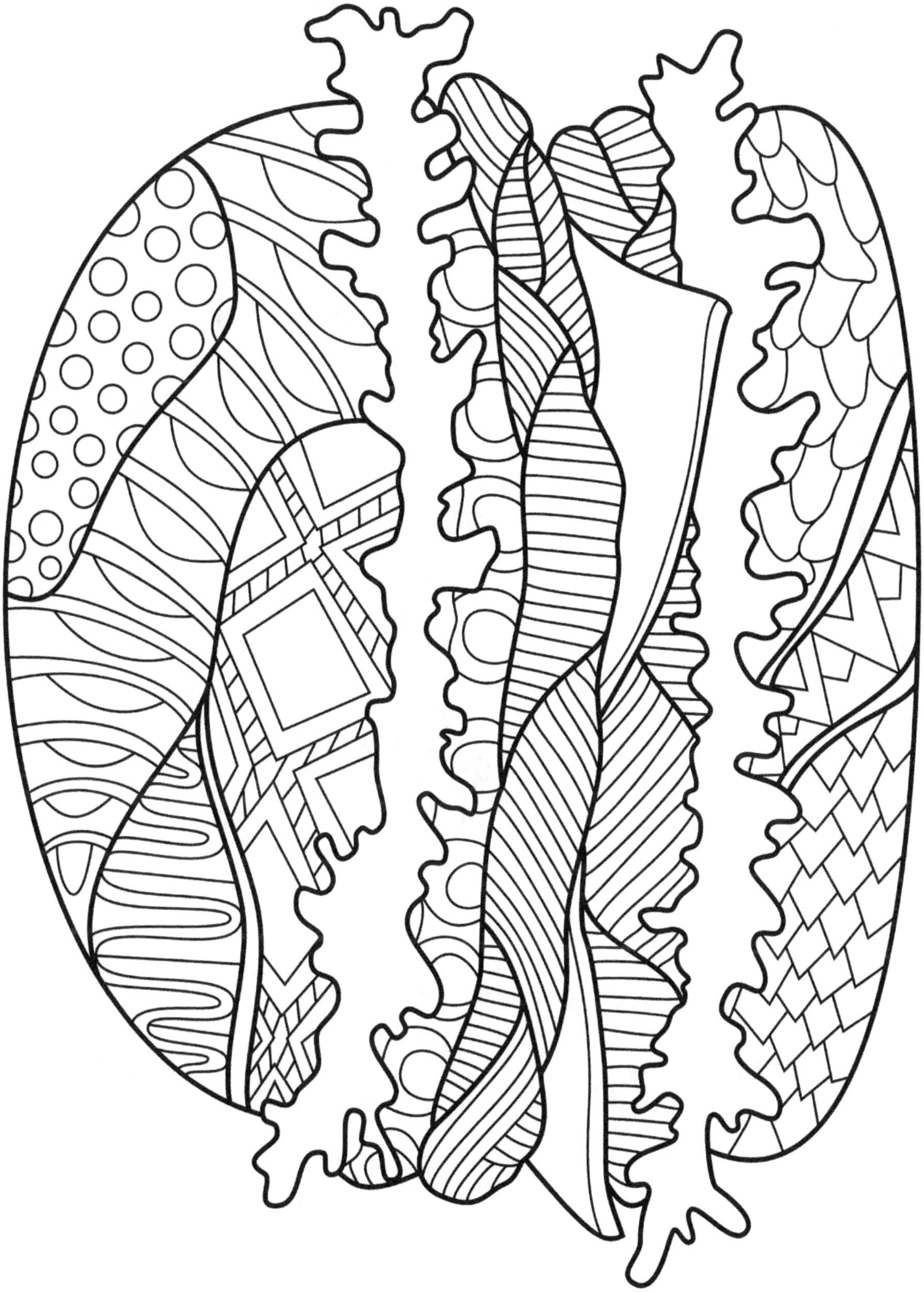

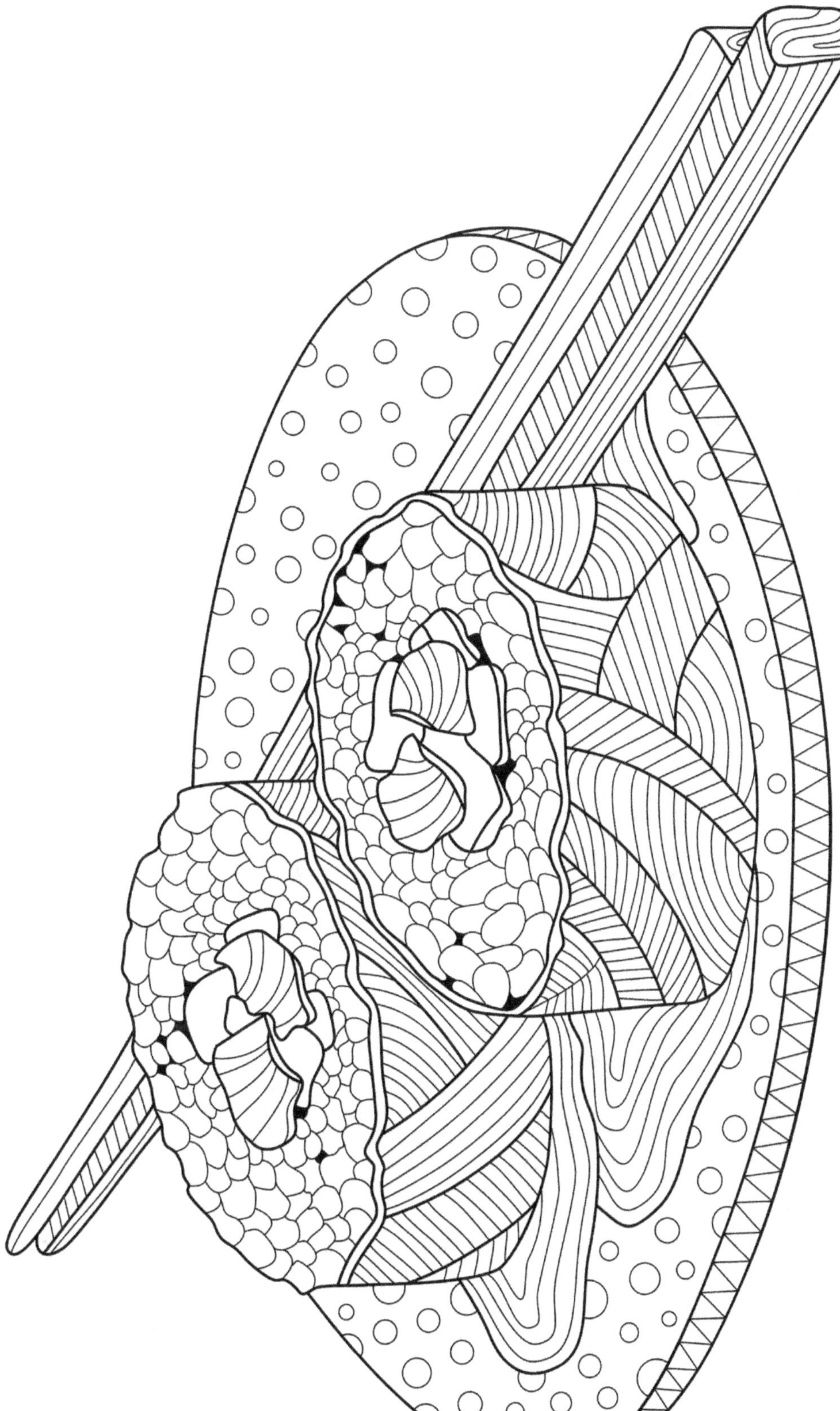

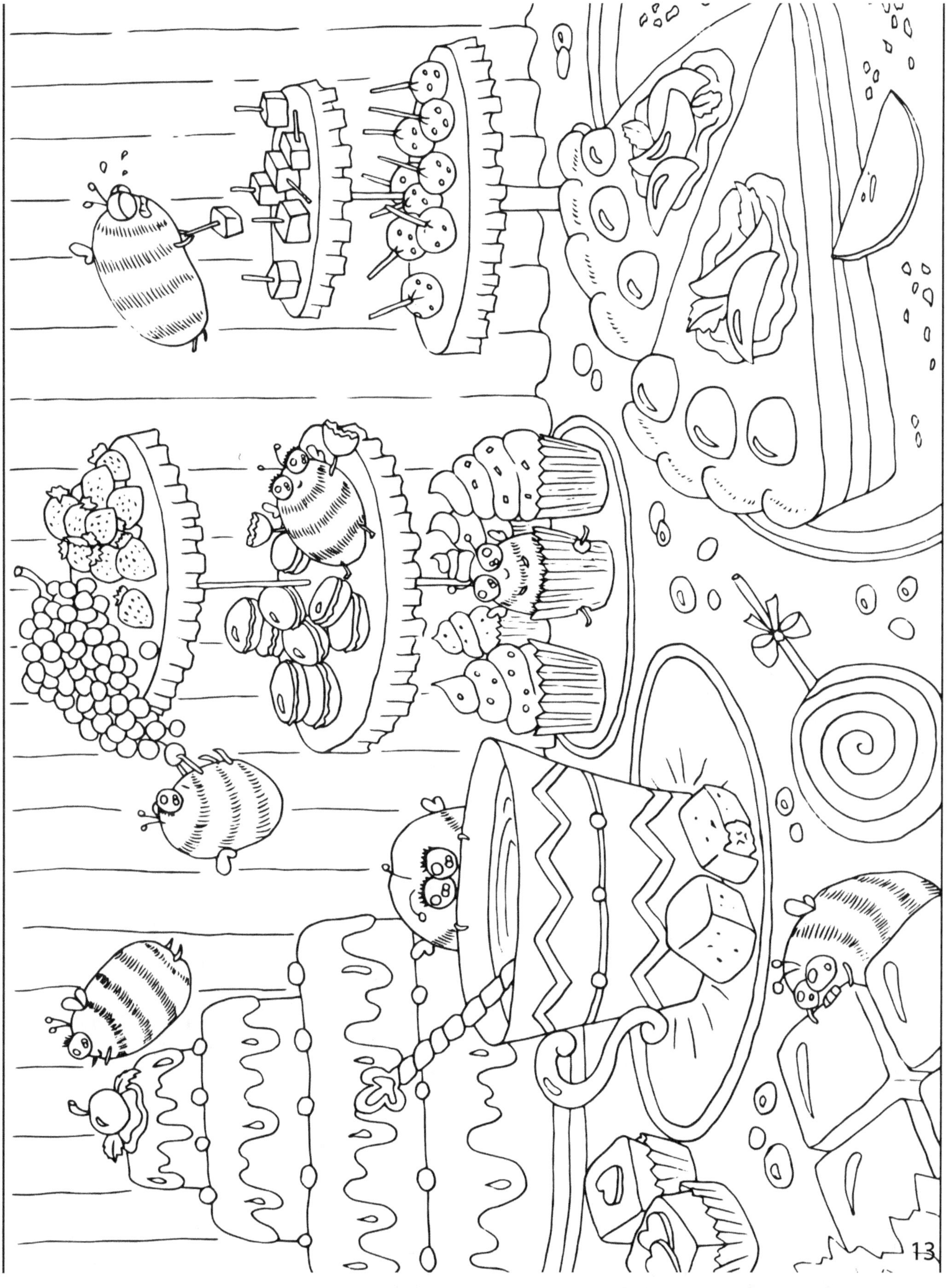

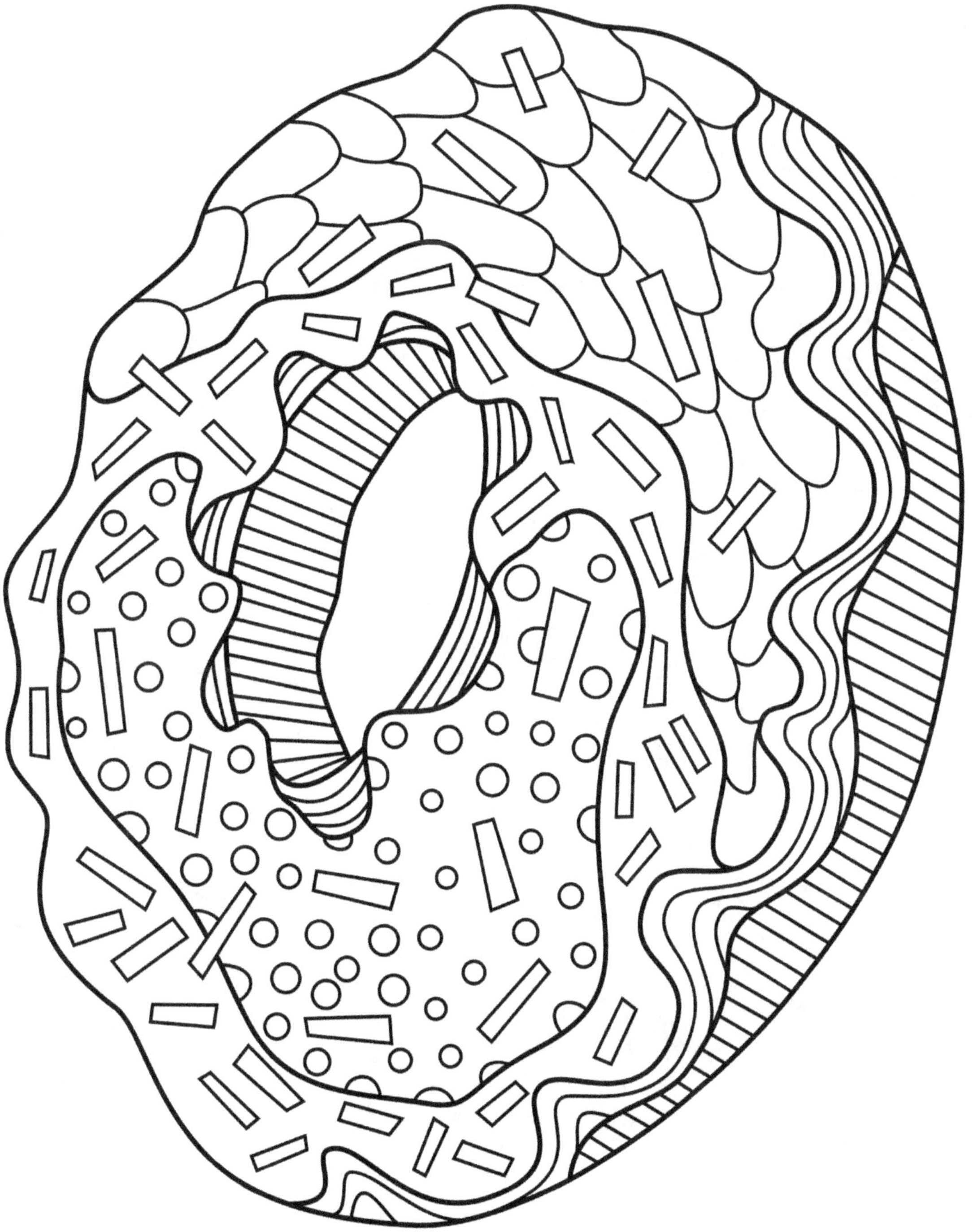

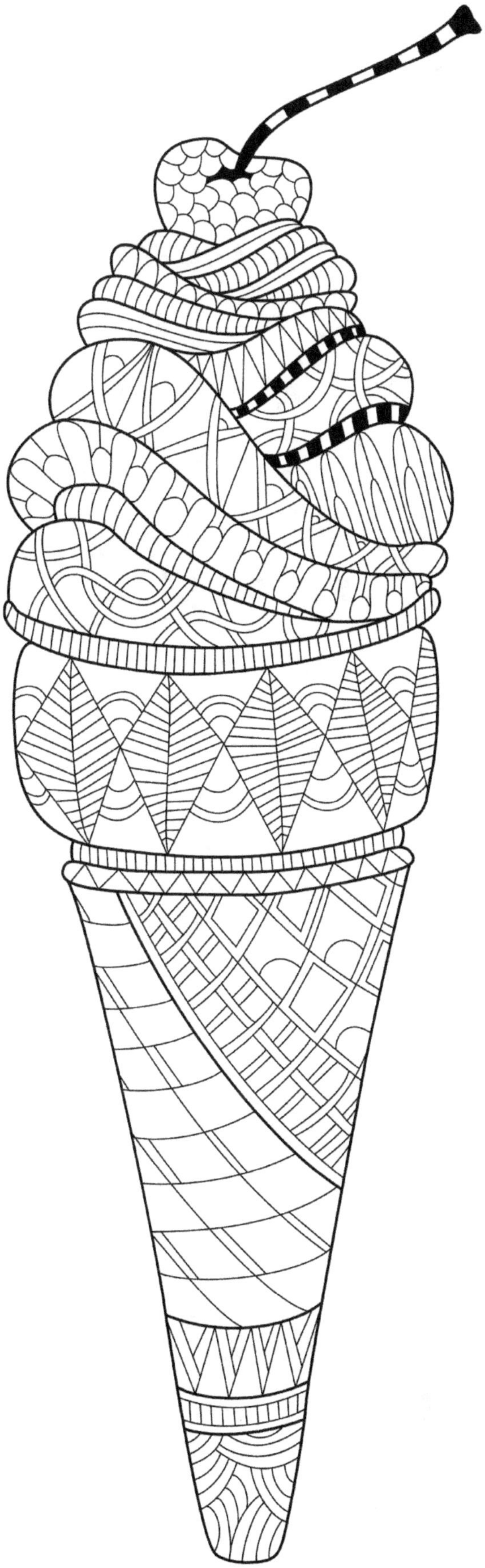

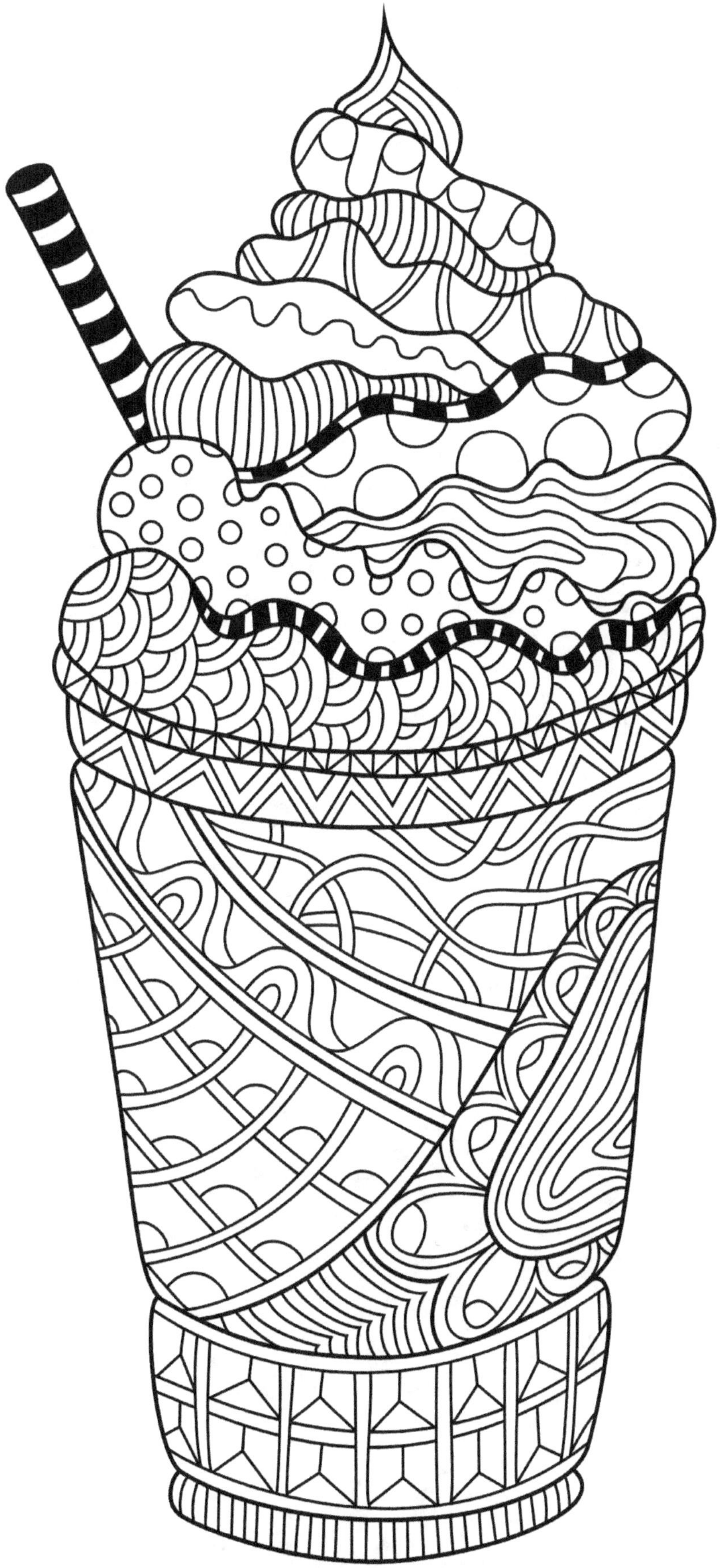

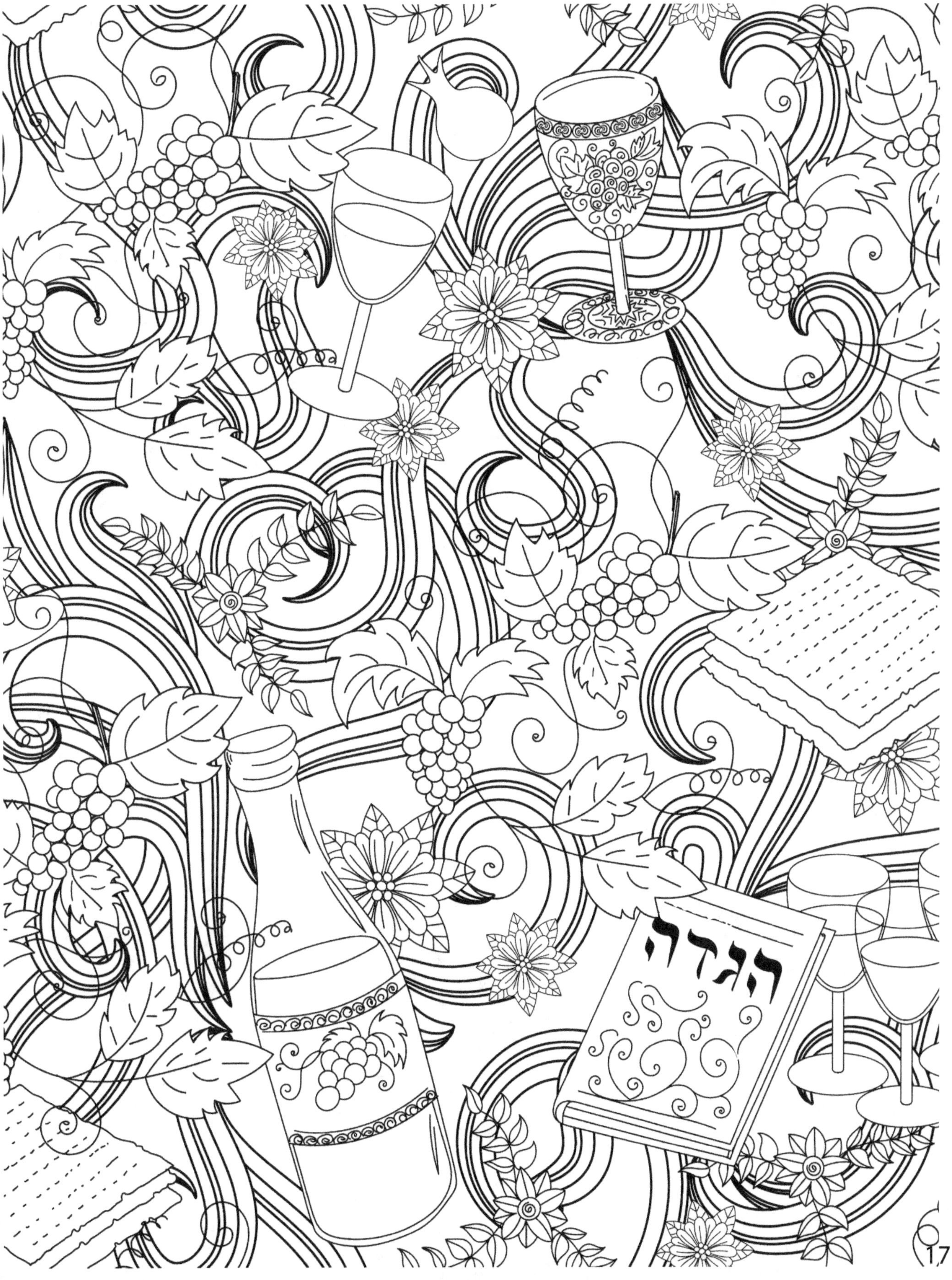
הגדה

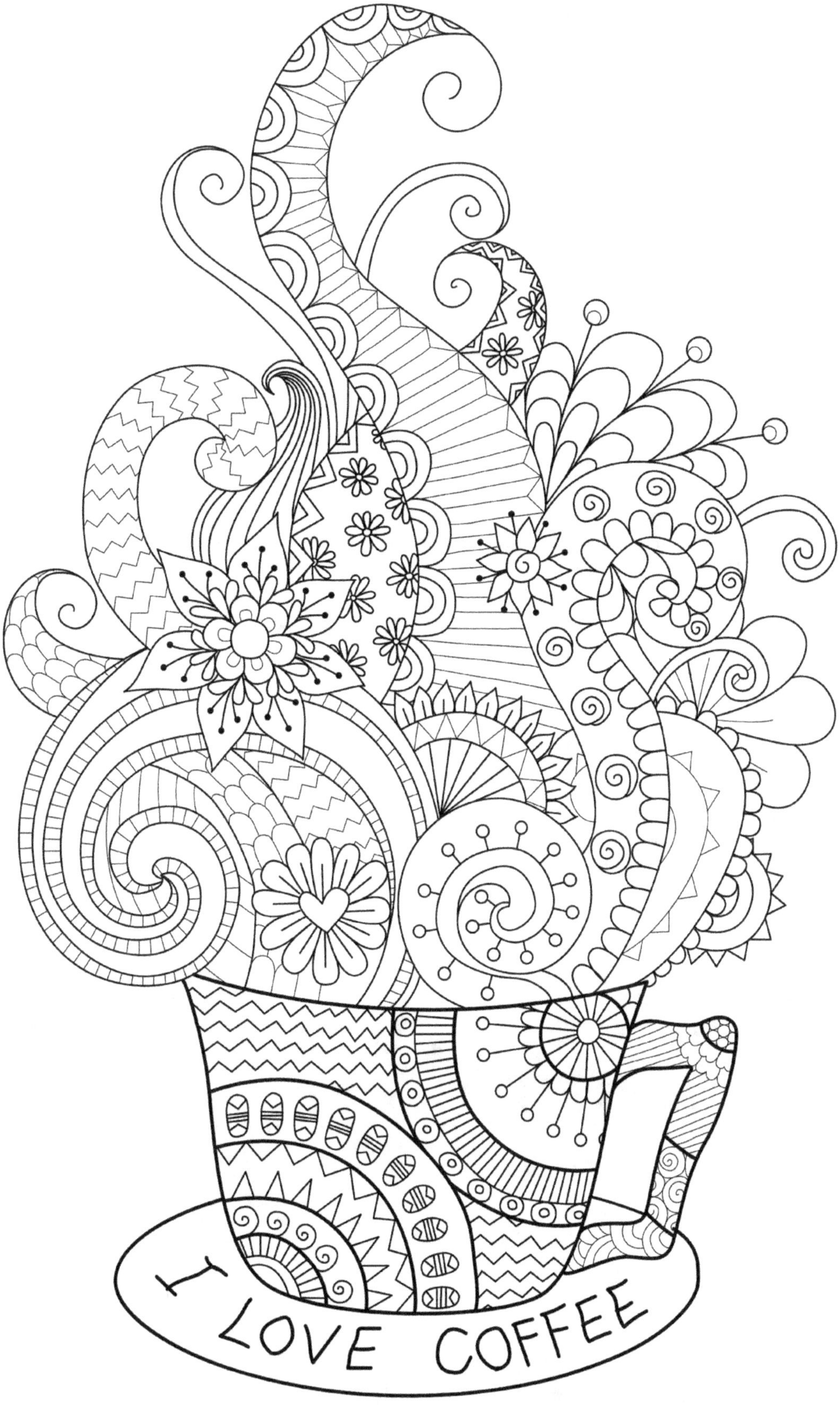
I LOVE COFFEE

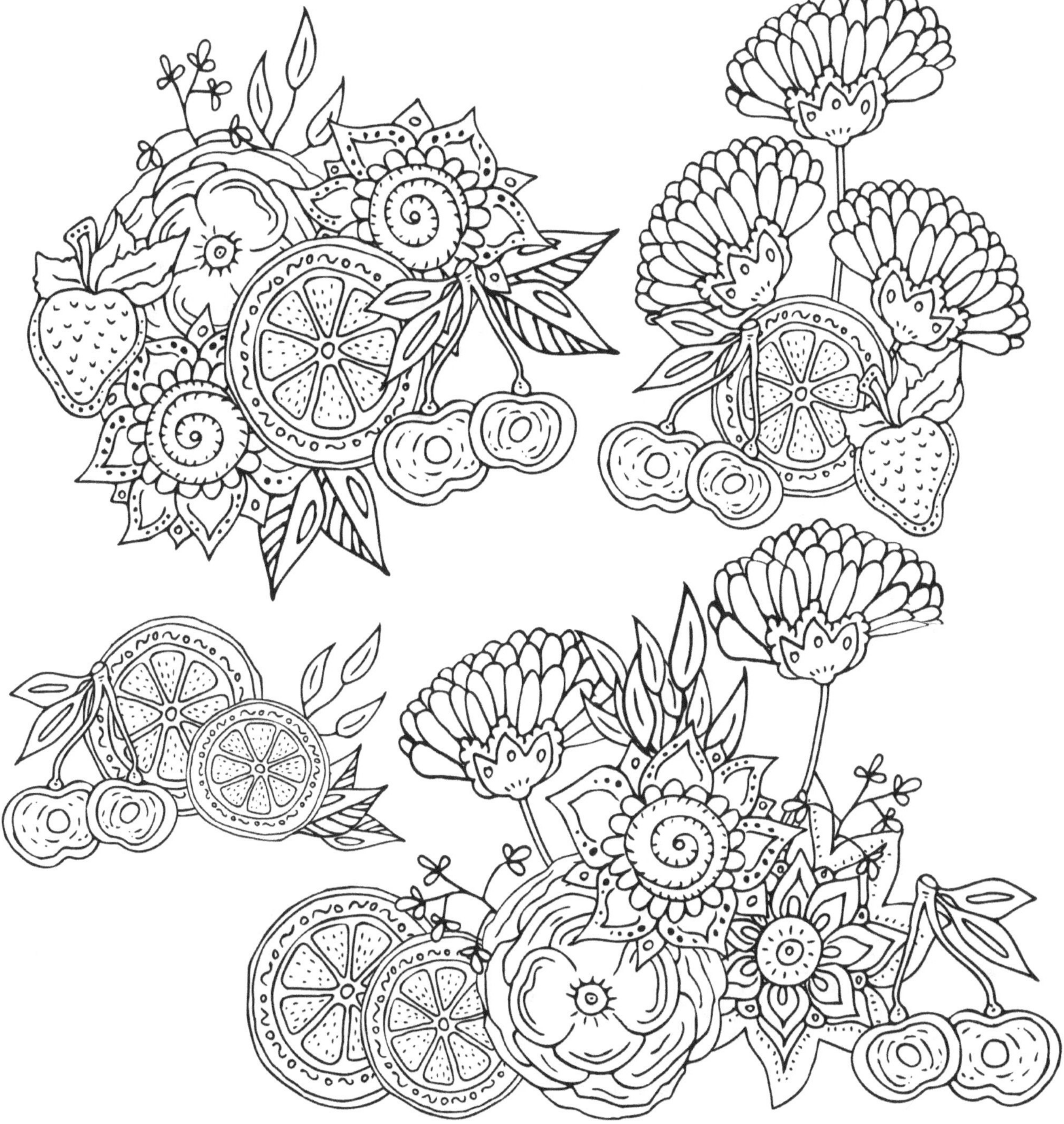

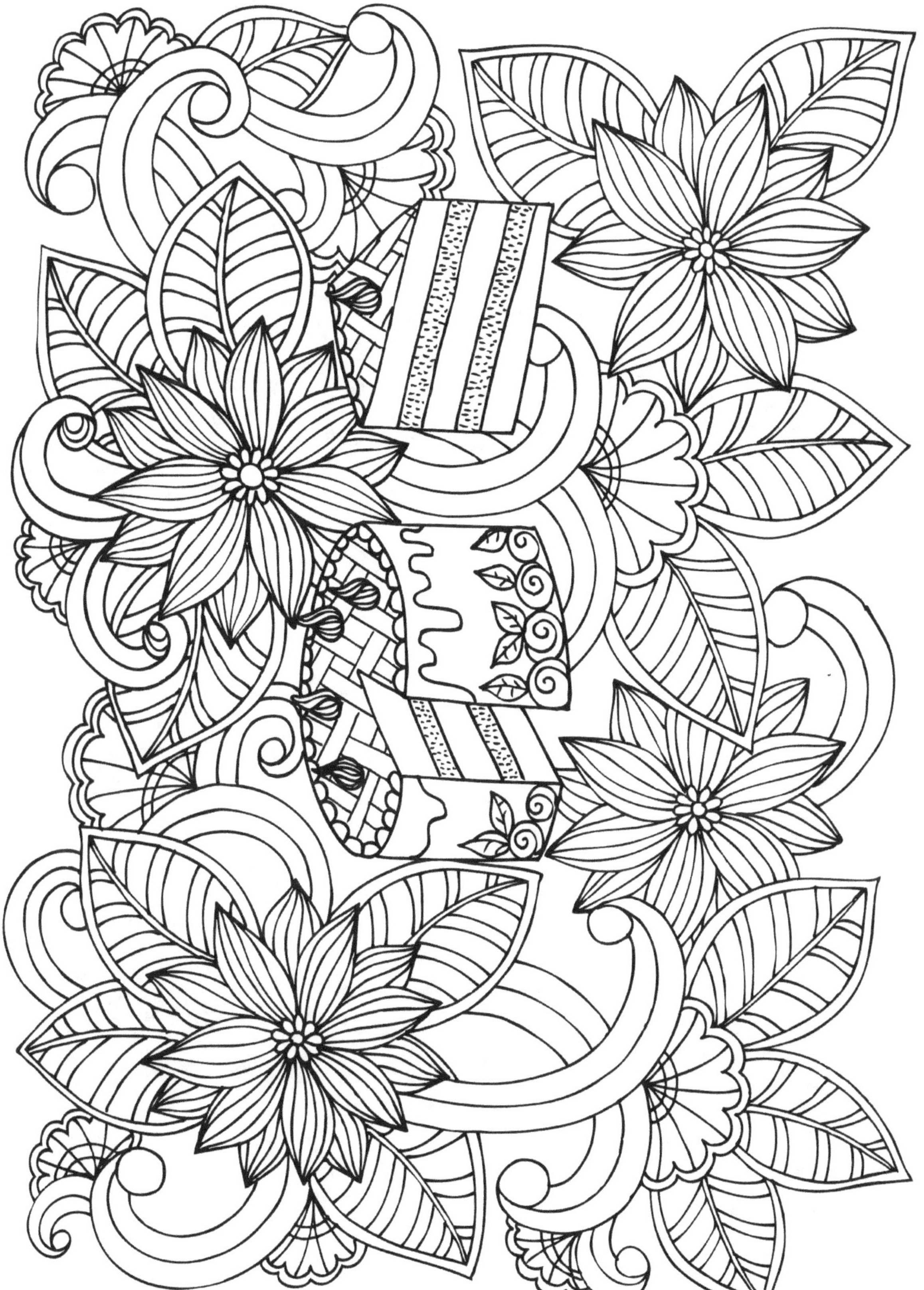

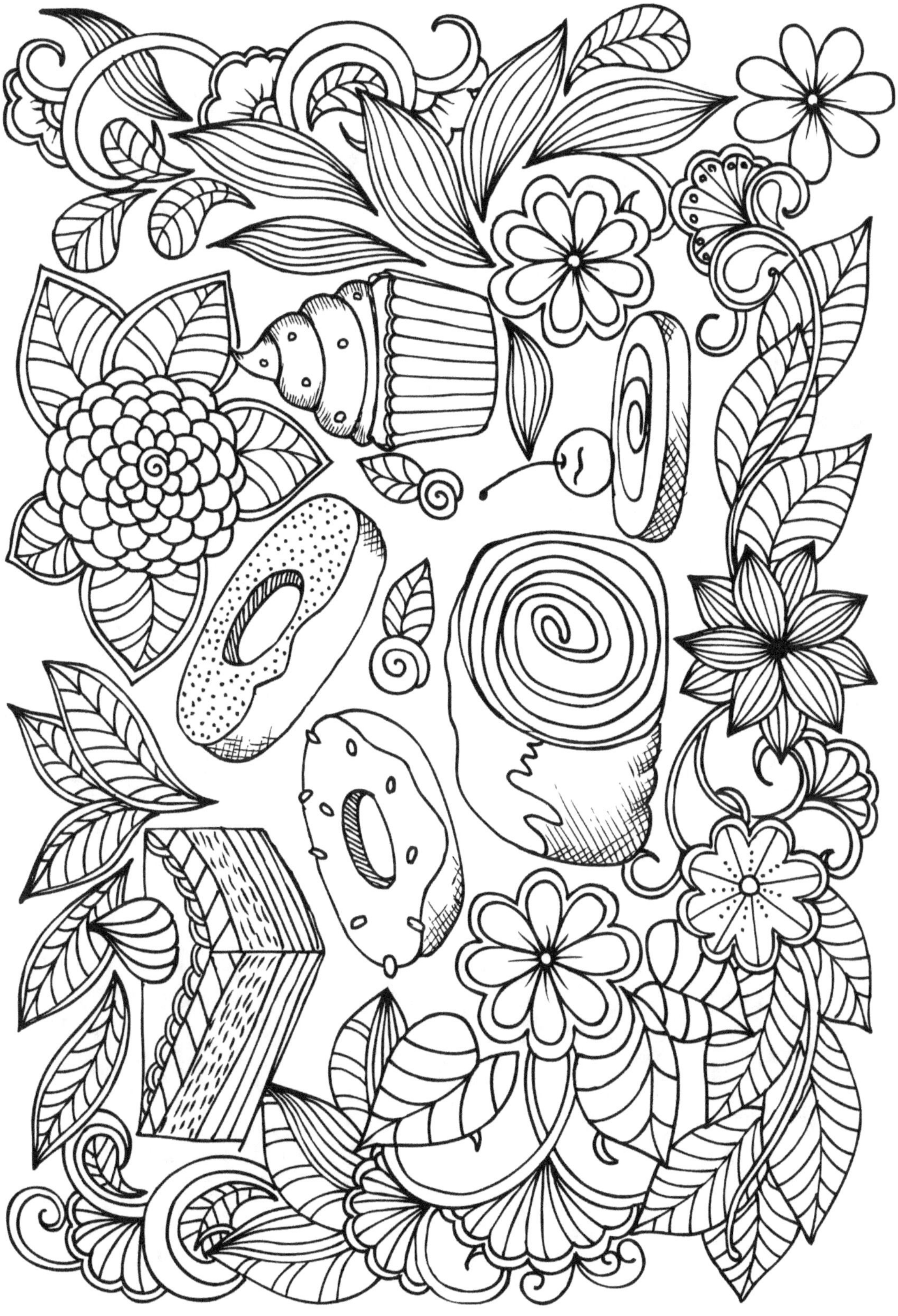

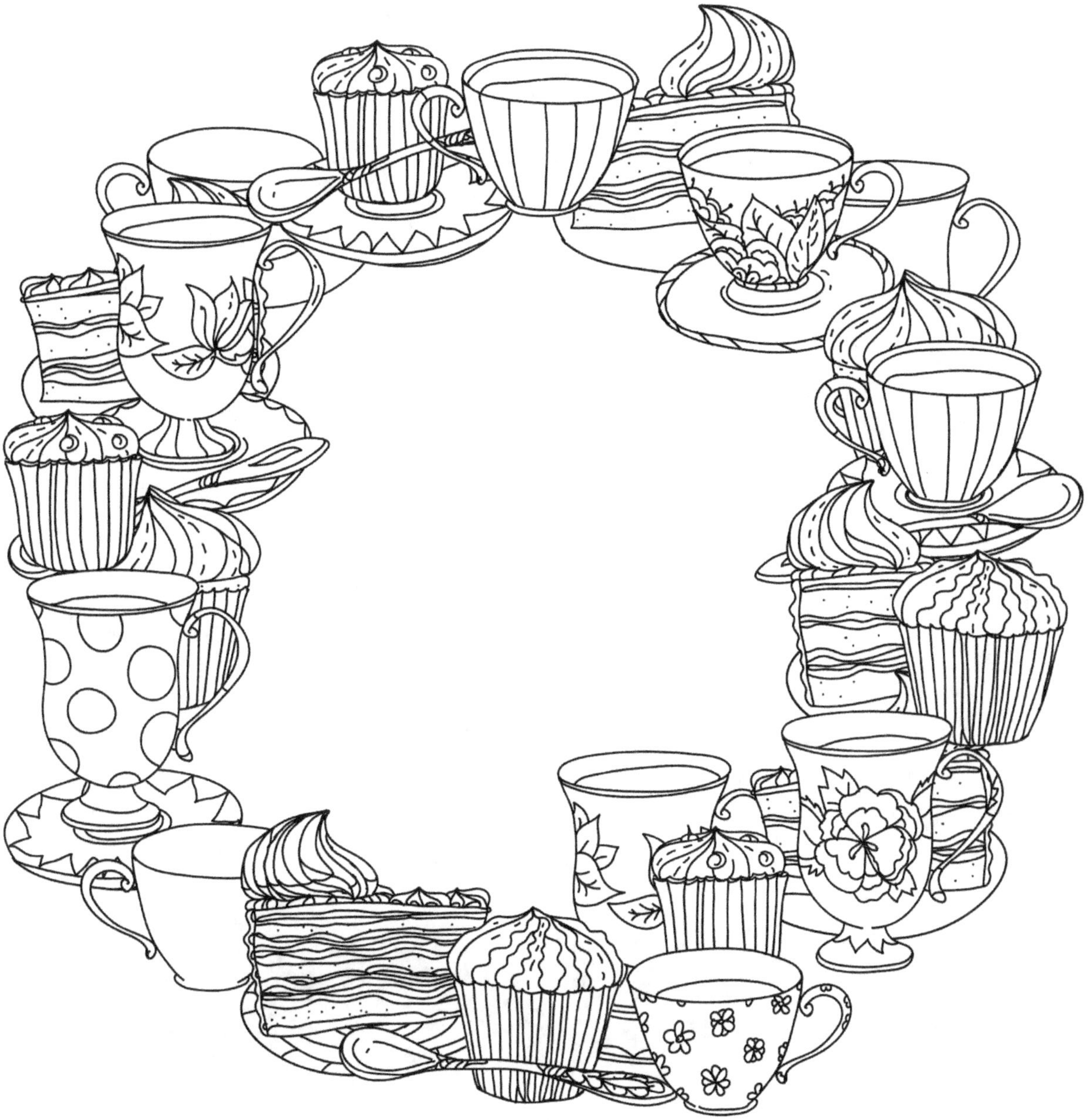

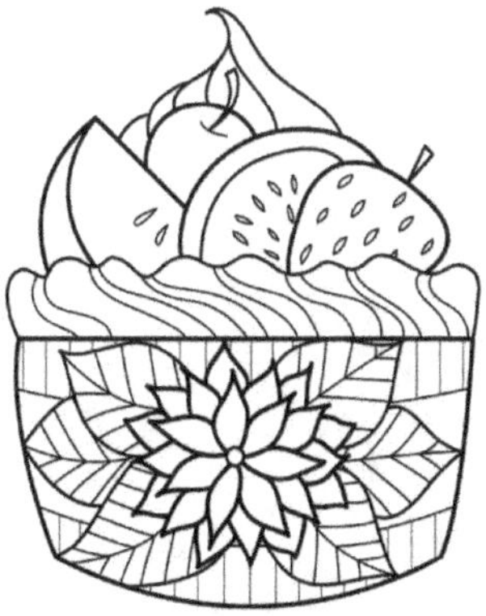
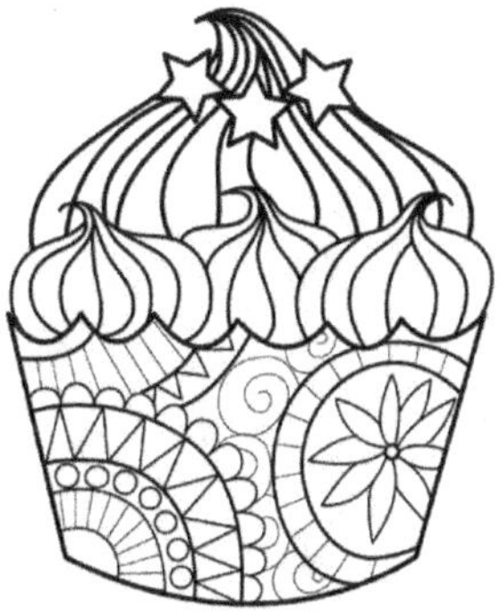
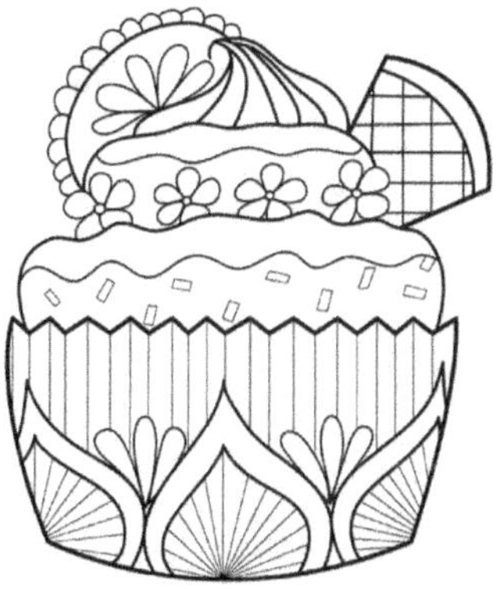
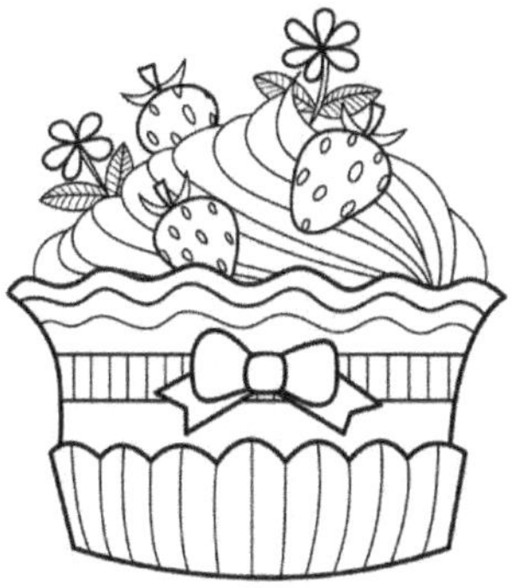

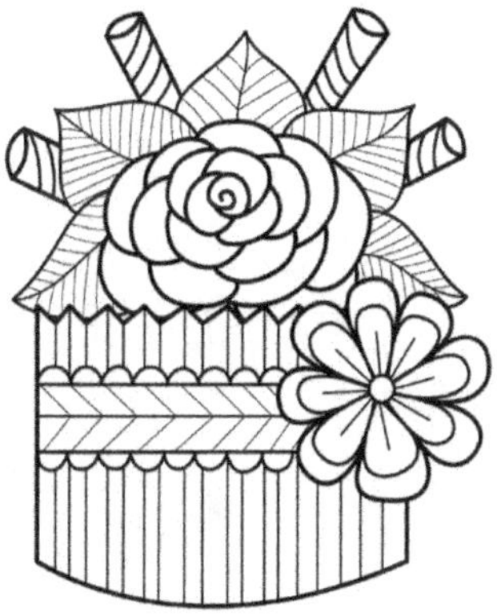
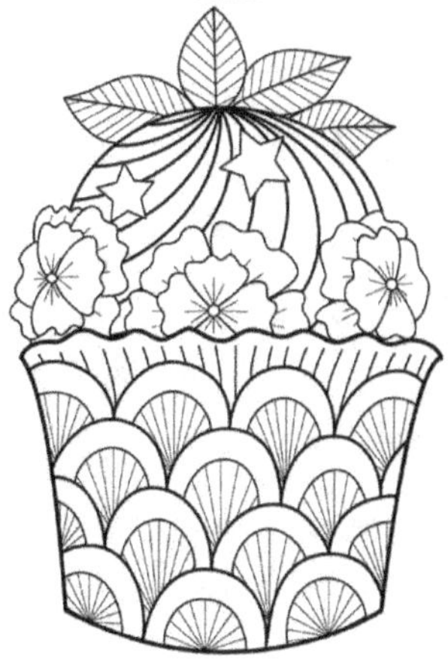

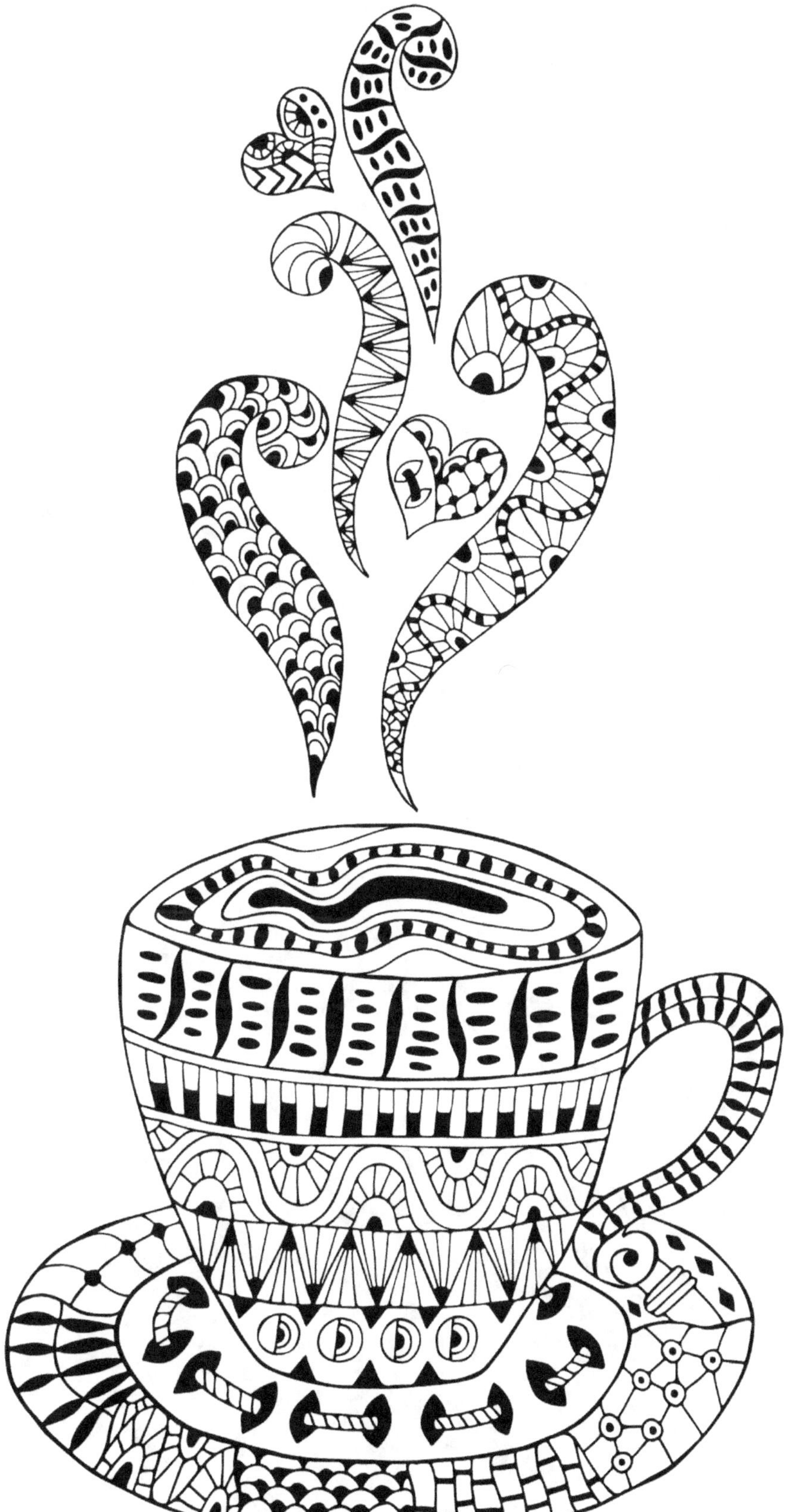

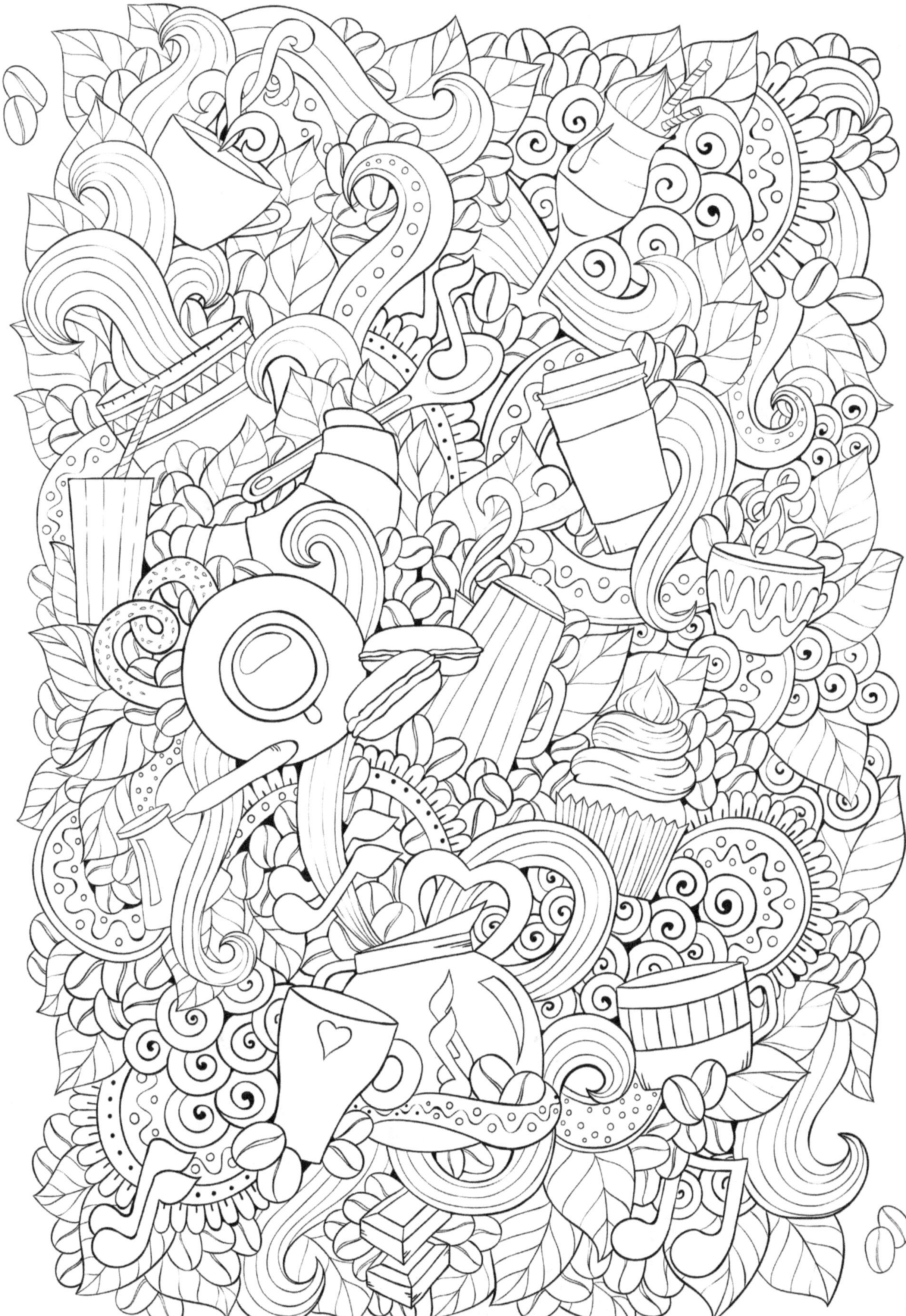

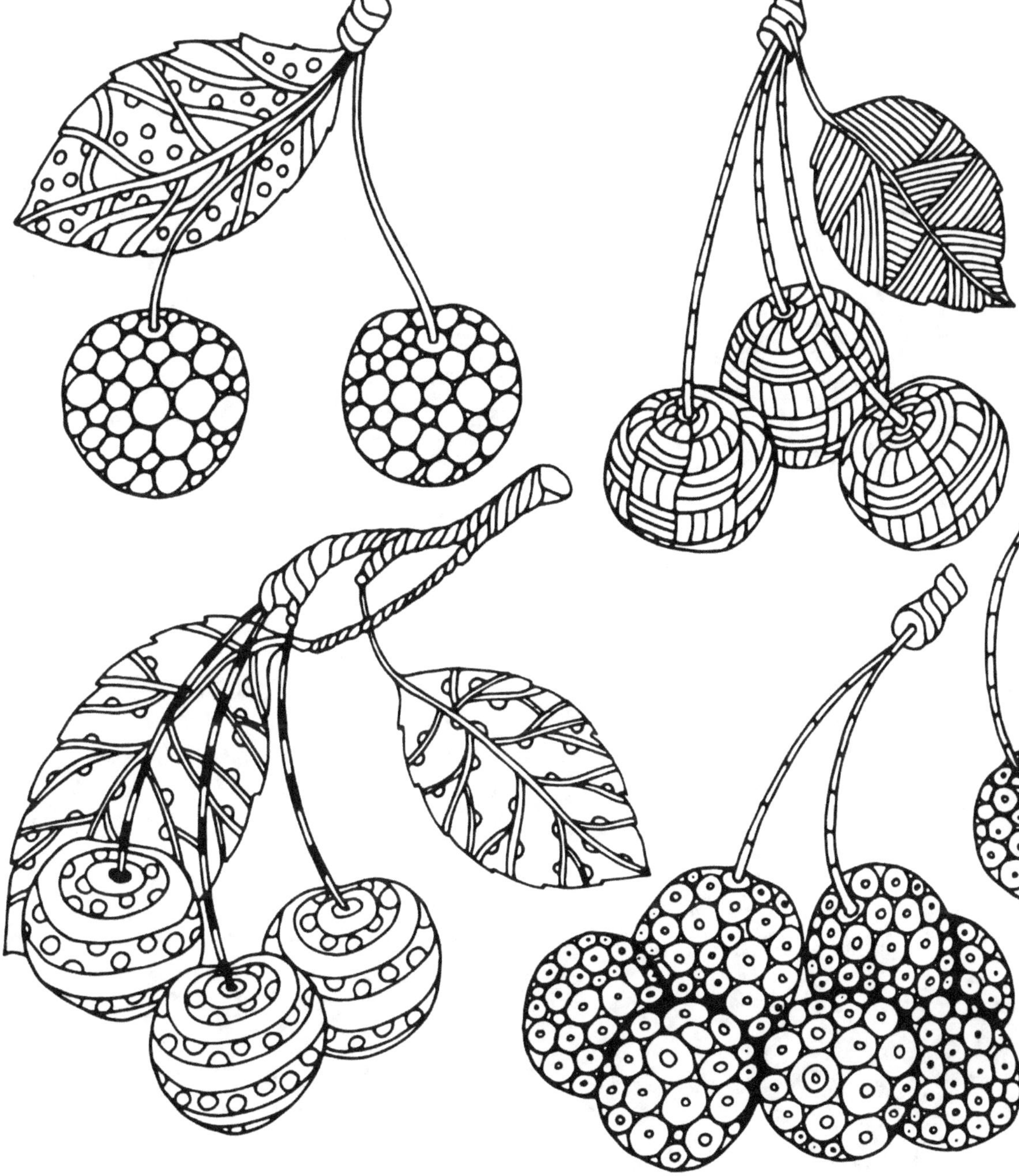

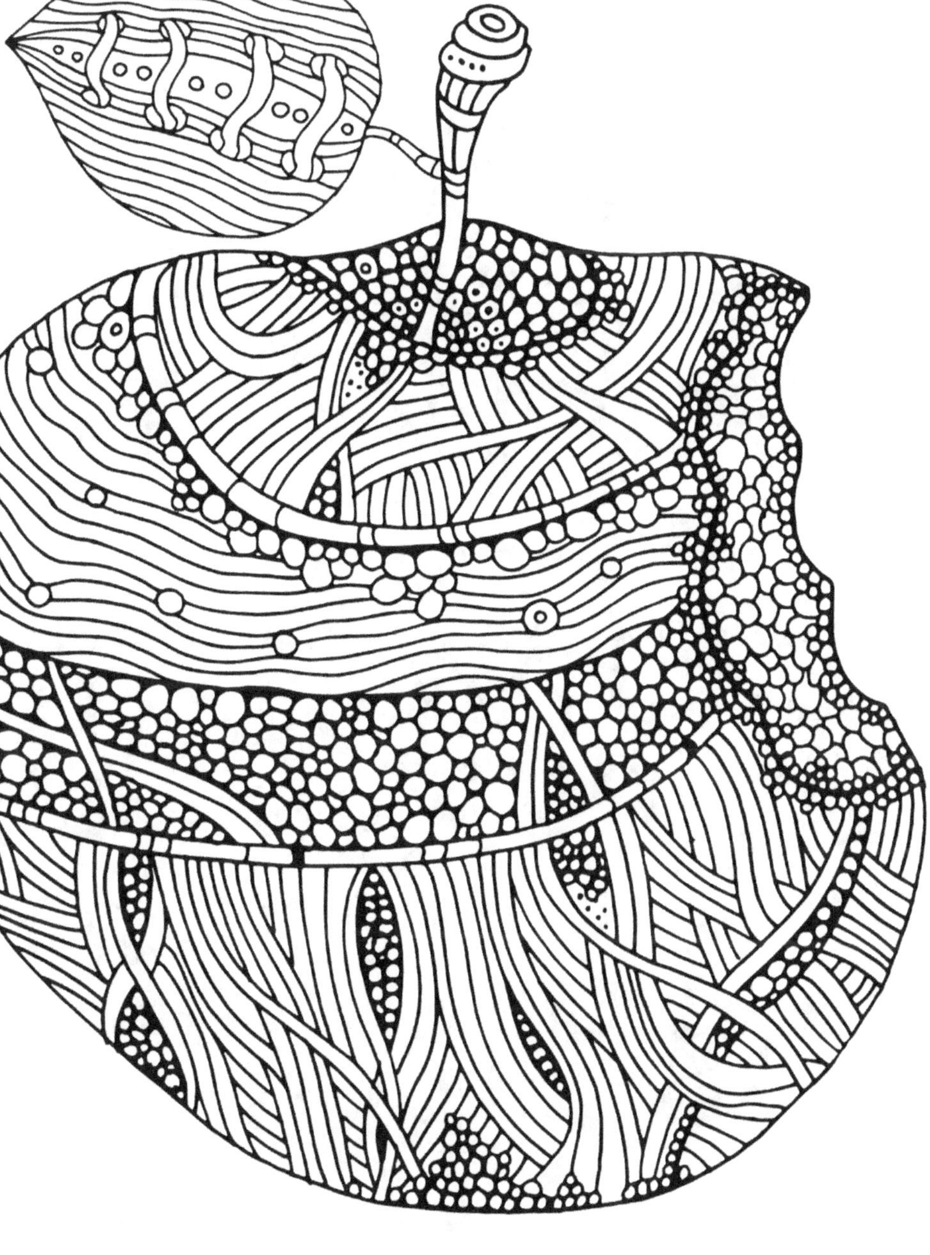

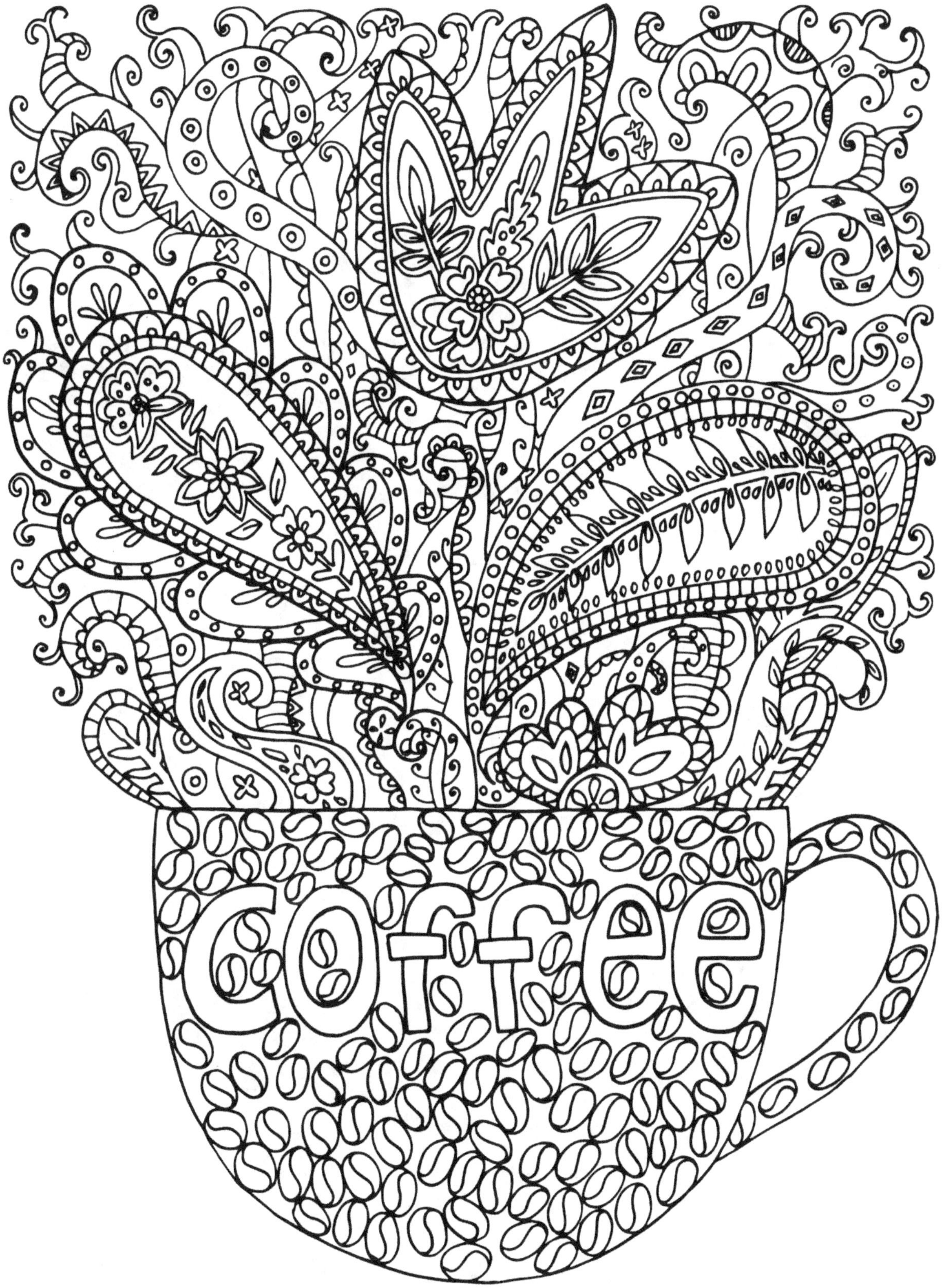
coffee

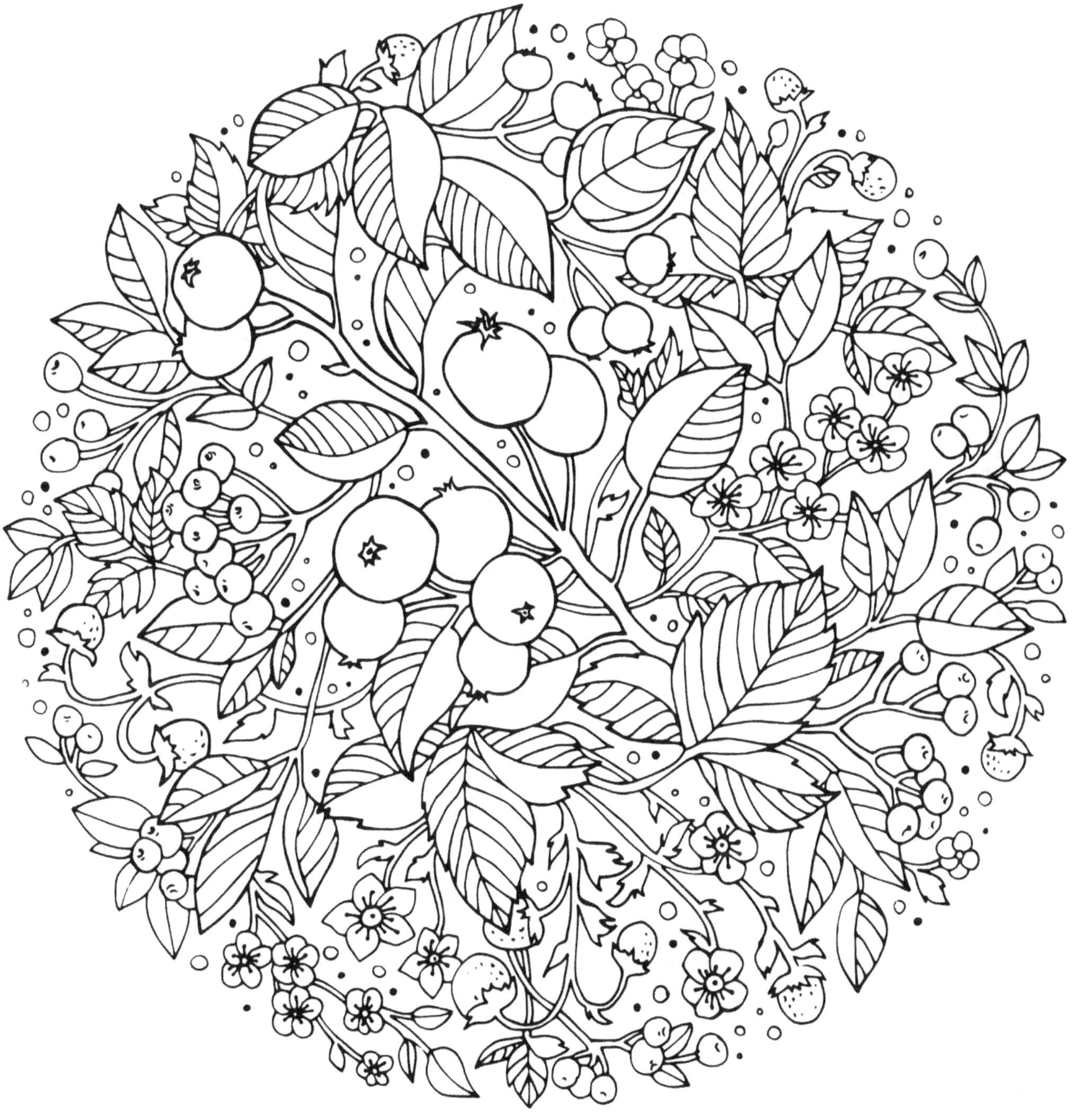

www.ingramcontent.com/pod-product-compliance
Lightning Source LLC
Chambersburg PA
CBHW081617220526
45468CB00010B/2914
* 9 7 8 1 9 4 2 9 1 5 5 8 4 *